TWO ARIAS
BY MOZART

arranged for B flat clarinet and piano

by A. W. BENOY and A. BRYCE

Voi che sapete (*The Marriage of Figaro*)
Ah, perdona (*Titus*)

MUSIC DEPARTMENT

OXFORD
UNIVERSITY PRESS

TWO ARIAS BY MOZART

for B flat Clarinet and Piano

Arranged by
A. W. BENOY & A. BRYCE

1. VOI CHE SAPETE

(The Marriage of Figaro)

★ The separate clarinet part is in B flat

Printed in Great Britain
OXFORD UNIVERSITY PRESS, MUSIC DEPARTMENT, GREAT CLARENDON STREET, OXFORD OX2 6DP

OXFORD MUSIC for clarinet

OXFORD

Two Arias by Mozart

arranged for B flat clarinet and piano

A.W. Benoy & A. Bryce

1. VOI CHE SAPETE
(The Marriage of Figaro)

Printed in Great Britain
OXFORD UNIVERSITY PRESS, MUSIC DEPARTMENT, GREAT CLARENDON STREET, OXFORD OX2 6DP

Two Arias by Mozart

Two Arias by Mozart

Two Arias by Mozart

2. AH, PERDONA
(Titus)

Two Arias by Mozart

Two Arias by Mozart

Processed and printed by
Halstan & Co. Ltd., Amersham, Bucks., England

OXFORD UNIVERSITY PRESS

Clarinet in B flat

2. AH, PERDONA
(Titus)

OXFORD UNIVERSITY PRESS

Oxford Music for Clarinet includes:

Bach arr. Lawton	Jesu, Joy of Man's Desiring
ed. Beechey	Five Romantic Pieces
	Six Romantic Pieces
arr. Benoy and Bryce	First Pieces for B flat Clarinet
Debussy arr. Lethbridge	Debussy for clarinet
arr. Frank and Forbes	Classical and Romantic Pieces
	Books 1 and 2
Jacob	Five Pieces
arr. Lawton	The Young Clarinettist
Lefèvre ed. Dobrée	Three Sonatas
ed. Davies and Harris	Five Sonatas
Mendelssohn arr. Benoy and Bryce	Two Songs Without Words
Moszkowski arr. Lethbridge	Two Spanish Dances
Mozart arr. Benoy and Bryce	Two Arias
arr. Douglas	Minuet and Trio
Rossini arr. Hermann ed. Glazer	Introduction, Theme, and Variations
Walton arr. Palmer	A Clarinet Album

OXFORD UNIVERSITY PRESS

ISBN 0-19-357838-7

9 780193 578388